WAR STRATEGY DIVERGENCE PLACE CULTURES ON A COLLISION COURSE

> The growth of the power of Athens, and the alarm which this inspired in Sparta, made war inevitable.

> —Thucydides[1]

Uncertainty is the central reality of the current and foreseeable strategic horizon. The world's power balance is in transition as China emerges from its self imposed isolationism in the first 30 years of the People's Republic. China's emergence has resulted in its ascendancy as a modern global power akin with the U.S. relative decline despite its continuing hegemonic supremacy. At the same time, impelled by new security challenges and changing economic realities, and not least a new realignment of relative political and economic influence between them, both countries are engaged in searching debates about domestic purposes, their world roles and ultimately their relation to each other.[2] General George C. Marshall wrote this in mid-1925 about China when he was stationed there; "politically it is the most interesting problem in the world today, and the most dangerous."[3] Nearly one hundred years later the same can be written.

The growing story of the United States-China rivalry for influence globally already dominates popular and academic discourse. "Indeed, a 'China threat' debate quickly emerged to dominate U.S. and Western discussion of international politics and policy considerations toward China."[4] The debate quickly escalated because "the United States and China have been not so much nation-states as continental expressions of cultural identities."[5] It is commonly shared that cultural identities shape the way people think and behave. Particularly, cultural identities shape world views, and influence the way people relate with the world at large. So, it is not unforeseen that national policies and their efforts on behalf of mankind can become points of friction. So "factors such as geopolitics and ideological differences make the military dimension of strategic competition inevitable and unavoidable."[6] It would be prudent to examine if there are any fundamental cultural differences on our perceptions of warfare?

This paper examines whether a new approach to intellectual discourse is applicable to the international security dialogue around the U.S.-China relations. The examination assesses whether strategic war cultures are the fundamental underpinnings to the manner in which these two rival nation states interact. Analysis will review historical and contemporary strategic documents; assess their correlation to current diplomatic, military, and economic involvement by the Chinese as it relates to their relationship with the United States and alliance partners; and concludes as to the impact of this correlation on current policies. An understanding of the historical and theoretical sources of war is essential to the development of a valid conceptual framework on which to base United States future engagement strategy with China.

An engagement strategy is difficult to embark on when there is an underlying stratum of distrust. In a classic Yin and Yang duality, a certain amount of distrust is good in the international arena because each nation have their own interests to serve; yet, a certain level of trust is the necessary lifeblood to any strategic relationship in order to develop mutual cooperation and support. Any grand strategy that assumes that no one wants war, and that everybody is either satisfied with the status quo or can be made so by diplomatic means leaves that country vulnerable to any government that disagrees.[7] Paraphrasing the Nobel laureate, Elihu Root, strategic diligence is not about promoting war, but it is about the preservation of peace through intelligent and adequate preparation to repel aggression to achieve the right balance in order to prevent strategic surprise.

Trust is difficult to build when we define the U.S.-China relationship within the constraints of a pendulum swing where one end is labeled competitor and the other end is adversary. Along that definitional continuum, there is not much maneuver space between rival—threat--enemy. Conversely, "foreigners in the eyes of Chinese are inferior, corrupt, decadent, disloyal and volatile, frequently hegemonic, barbaric and, in essence, 'devils.'"[8] This cultural view is predicated on how China sees itself among nations. "China sees herself as the middle kingdom, the center of the universe and the world's oldest culture and society."[9] These basic views of each other create a fundamental level of mistrust and can be the basis for an initial adversarial relationship to fester. However, a more accurate underpinning for the legacy of distrust stems from the Cold War experience where the United States took a pro-democracy stance and painted the Communists as a system that need to be overthrown.

"While we are not using the term 'enemy' or suggesting that our relationship is adversarial, one cannot deny the fact that our countries have divergent political philosophies, and that a very real competition for resources and alliances exists."[10] It is recognized that we have diametrically opposed political ideologies (Democracy vice Communism). Additionally, that China has a growing appetite for natural resources to feed its economic juggernaut and a growing military modernization program puts it in direct competition against the United States for the accumulation of dwindling worldwide resources to maintain its own economic strength that finances its military supremacy. We have a lop-sided co-dependency with China for goods, services, and production, and we need to set boundaries. "China is also back to double-digit defense spending increases exceeding $90 billion for 2011."[11]

That China has shrewdly found a way to strategically establish a significant footprint in the exploitation of natural resources from Africa and South America and in turn leveraged this economic foothold into an opportunity to become a key strategic player in those regions. This has increased the propensity for disagreements to develop. "But disagreements should not prevent cooperation on issues of mutual interest, because a pragmatic and effective relationship between the United States and China is essential to address the major challenges of the 21st century."[12]

We must understand the relevance of culture in policy and strategy formulation and outcome. The greatest risk in development of a pragmatic and effective relationship in the international environment is an unlimited prospect for cultural conflict. There is "something that the West would do well to remember, given our congenital illusion that anyone who shares aspects of our culture must necessarily agree with our foreign policy."[13] Conflict over foreign policy can happen across the diplomatic, military and economic elements of power. Cross cultural savvy is a critical requirement when operating in the international environment, but more so when the understanding deficit is related to the military element of power. Legitimacy is coin of the realm within the International Community when it comes to the use of military power.

In order to evaluate the divergent national views of war and strategy, we must use strategic thought processes to evaluate the national security challenges and opportunities facing the United States in the 21st century and synthesize critical elements, enablers, and processes that define the strategic environment in peace and war. The discussion of war is not done frivolously and the intent is not to undermine world security by having these discussions. One of America's greatest weaknesses is its failure to grasp the most basic weapon of all: understanding.[14]

We know of Pax Romana and Pax Britannica as historical memories. There are heard "whispers within the walls" that Pax Americana is in decline. Pax Americana provided stabilization to the international community for nearly three quarters of a century since 1945 and it was done on the backbone strength of U.S. military power. A military power largely built through the evolution of United States strategy and tactics founded on historical and theoretical underpinnings.

The U.S. and War – An Image Indivisible

The United States has a reputation as a nation constantly at war. "Our history, in fact, is studded with conflict and violence. From the Revolution to the Cold War, Americans have been willing to fight for their interests, their beliefs, and their ambitions."[15]

As America was coalescing it was also shaping its United States military's tactics and strategies. America fought on the frontiers waging battle on shores of lakes, rivers, and woodlands occupied by Native American Indians and other European Powers who were trying to establish colonial claims or expand territory on their original claims. It was here that America began to educate itself about the conception of war. The lessons learned were adapted on a grander scale when it was needed in America's bid for self-determination. America as a nation was born as a result of victory in War. It was the first manifestation as a nation in its fight for Independence that American stood fast and declared we will fight for our interests, beliefs, and especially our ambitions.

George Washington first established the enduring legacy of the American hybrid "Way of War" using conventional and unconventional means. Destruction or annihilation was not an option for General Washington as a military strategist; He had to undertake a war of attrition and exhaustion to defeat the well trained British forces. He understood about attrition and exhaustion because that was the state of his forces whenever he engaged in a head-on fight with European Battlefield style tactics. He quickly adapted his forces to fight in a non-traditional manner and thereby reversed the battle equation through the attrition and exhaustion of the British forces until victory was achieved. The British forces never adapted to the American way of fighting which led to their defeat. It was at this moment that: "American military culture thus became a self-contradictory hybrid of form, restraint, and etiquette, on the one hand, improvisation, raw energy, and unwillingness to accept limits on the other."[16]

The intervening years between the American Revolutionary War and the American Civil War saw America expanding westward to the Pacific Ocean. Along the way they encountered American Indians who attempted to stem the encroachment on their lands. It was also here that America learned about annihilation. "The Indian campaigns early on encouraged the notion that the object of war is nothing less than the enemy's destruction as a military power."[17]

Then America fought its Civil War. It is the American Civil War which solidified how America would approach how it went to war. President Abraham Lincoln beseeched, cajoled General Meade and his Army of the Potomac to go out and engage the enemy and in particular destroy General Robert E. Lee's Army and sweep away any opposition. But the Cult of Napoleon was strong and President Lincoln met with opposition from his Military Generals who were reluctant to engage what they perceived as vastly superior numbers. "To this point, consequently, the mainstream of American strategy in thought and in action was cautious, an eighteenth-century rather than a Napoleonic kind of strategy, Jominian rather than Clausewitzian."[18] It was not until President Lincoln found General Ulysses S. Grant and placed him as the General of the Army that there came a change in the Tide of Battle and eventually the War. General Lee fought as a Napoleonic General but was no match to General Grant, who was an unapologetic annihilationist.

President Lincoln through his readings on military strategy became a Clausewitzian acolyte. He accepted that; "war is thus an act of force to compel our enemy to do our will."[19] Additionally, "Clausewitz stated that wars are of two kinds, those that seek the overthrow of the enemy, and those that seek merely to achieve some conquests on the frontiers of the enemy's country."[20] This is why President Lincoln was so adamant about destroying the enemies will to fight and would not negotiate. President Lincoln had two firm end state goals that would never be a term for negotiation during the War between the North and South: 1) Preserve the Union at all costs; and 2) Abolish Slavery. To accomplish this in a true Clausewitzian manner he had to destroy the Rebel military force to compel compliance.

The successful preservation of the Union created a temporary amnesiac effect in American military strategic thought with a total disregard for military history before the Civil War. This started a historical legacy that carried into the continued westward expansion of the continental United States and the subsequent attempted extermination of the American Indian to a more modern example of the War on Terror, where the total

destruction of Al Qaeda is the stated political objective.

> In the history of American strategy, the direction taken by the American conception of war made most American strategists, through most of the time span of American history, strategists of annihilation. At the beginning, when American military resources were still slight, America made a promising beginning in the nurture of strategists of attrition; but the wealth of the country and its adoption of unlimited aims in war cut that development short, until the strategy of annihilation became characteristically the American way in war.[21]

Nevertheless, until the onset of World War II, America fairly operated on its own,

until it was necessary to fight in a coalition of allies. Winston Churchill captured it best

with his comment on the America's entry into World War II "the only thing worse than

fighting a war with allies is fighting a war without them". Until then America had

principally two kinds of strategies: annihilation and attrition through exhaustion. And "as

time went on and the military power of the United States grew greater, Americans with

increasing frequency fought wars of Clausewitz's first type, to overthrow the enemy."[22]

America became a fanatical adherent to the Clausewitzian postulation that "war is

merely the continuation of policy by other means."[23] It was the genesis of the leveraging

of scientific and technological breakthroughs with military implications to affect the

desired outcomes of war. This was war on a grand scale with destructive power never

seen before. General Lemay's carpet bombing programs in Europe and on the

Japanese mainland culminating with the usage of the first and only application of atomic

bombs on the cities of Hiroshima and Nagasaki, Japan. This wanton destruction was

not simply contributory to the final objective of the strategist; it was in itself an intrinsic

part of that objective. "It was ultimately, to use a commercial analogy, the only thing that would show up on the final balance sheet of war."[24] Even here Clausewitz had a ready answer for the annihilation strategist to justify the ferocity of war.

> Clausewitz recognized that every age had its own kind of war. A new theory of war emerges as a result of a combination of drastic change in the international security environment, diplomacy, domestic politics, ideology, economics, and revolutionary advances in technology.[25]

This led to a new strategic effort during the Cold War. It was a battle of political ideologies and goals. Clausewitz had reached his ascendancy in American strategic thought and the conviction held forth was; "the political object is the goal, war is the means of reaching it, and means can never be considered in isolation from their purpose."[26] That is why American diplomacy has been branded as Gunboat Diplomacy, Coercive Diplomacy, Muscular Diplomacy, and Band-Aid Diplomacy,

The Policy of Containment and the Deterrence Strategy blended operational and strategic art that Russian forces had used so successfully to counter the Clausewitzian strategy driven German Armies of World War II. A new end game had begun with the threat of the destruction of the world played out by two superpowers with the capability to annihilate the earth through Atomic Warfare.

However, increasingly the United States is challenged whenever they choose to juggle interests over values. This happened during the Vietnam War when we chose a strategy of annihilation over our interests and subjugated our values in what has now come to be viewed as an unjust war. The United States lost legitimacy and credibility as a consequence. And another big lesson learned was that political authorities must provide information sharing with the American public, an honest presentation of the risks, and do it with integrity.

The Gulf War sent a thunderclap notice to world of how technically advanced and capable our military forces had become and there was no peer competitor on the horizon. Now, fighting the War on Terror for the last ten years has reinforced our technological superiority but also highlighted our vulnerabilities to asymmetrical threats. A new debate over the existence of a revolution in military affairs and the validity of study and analysis as it relates to the conduct of war is now underway especially in a fiscally constrained environment. "For nearly two decades, the strategic environment has called for innovation and adaptation, but the United States response has been more bureaucratic 'business as usual' than thoughtful—even if iterative—change."[27] This has put us at risk as China has closed the strategic gap.

That is why we are now in preparatory stages to concentrate on the next threat and if necessary in order to preserve United States interests be prepared to go to war. America's focus has shifted to the Pacific Basin. "Since 1945, the nation has been engaged in two limited wars in Asia with disappointing outcomes"[28] and it is now preparing itself for a possible third. To recap our record for this area the count is zero wins, one loss, and one draw.

Americans do keep score and they like higher numbers in the win column and preferably zero losses. "United States political and military leaders are familiar with games such as chess, poker, boxing, and American football. These games to a large extent reflect and in turn influence American culture, strategic thinking, and the American way of war."[29] Therefore it is understandable that they are relevant to our definitions of how we describe war. In American culture, many compare the American way of war and diplomacy to the games of chess (power-based fight), poker (bluffing and risk-taking), boxing (force on force), and American football (in many ways, resembles the American war machine).[30]

America is recognizing that they are already engaged in a power-based fight and while its focus has been on the Middle East for the last two decades their risk-taking in the Asia-Pacific area is more than bluffing and may involve a need for a future force on force action that the American war machine may be unprepared to fight.

"The underpinning for the Pacific strategy reorientation was initiated by a study started by an Air Force and Navy task force committee more than two years ago that resulted in a concept called AirSea Battle."[31] The foundation for AirSea Battle focused "on the current multilayered threat to established trade routes by China and growing friction stemming from several territorial disputes that China has with neighboring countries."[32]

Our strategy states "We will support whole-of-nation deterrence approaches that blend economic, diplomatic, and military tools to influence adversary behavior."[33] Right now our strategic interests are primarily economic, but six of the world's largest militaries in this backyard make it a volatile, uncertain, complex, and ambiguous corner of the world. Our diplomatic and information efforts will need to convince a cynical Beijing that this adjustment in United States foreign policy that recognizes the economic boom in the Asia-Pacific region is not aimed at containment due to the rise of China. China on the other hand needs to persuade the United States and many other Asian nations such as Japan, Vietnam, and Taiwan no fear is warranted because of its two decade military buildup.

Retired Admiral Michael Mullen stated the following: "The Pacific Region is a critical economic region, a critical trade region and so I've gone from being curious about where China's headed to being concerned about it."[34] Recall what was said about sole reliance on diplomacy to secure a nation, it now makes that nation vulnerable to a nation that may have other less well meaning intentions. "The American military's propensity to view China as the 'enemy' may lead to a self-fulfilling prophecy."[35] But self-fulfilling prophecies can change through initial small efforts of engagement. "The United States can help change the zero sum narrative regarding United States-Chinese competition by focusing first on stability-enhancing projects that yield relatively simple wins."[36] However, changes to strategic culture will require time to affect the institutional nature of the United States military organization in order to understand how to achieve simple wins. "To support this, the Joint Force seeks a deeper military-to-military relationship with China to expand areas of mutual interest and benefit, improve understanding, reduce misperception, and prevent miscalculation."[37] The best message to be delivered in order to improve understanding, reduce misperception, and prevent miscalculation is about the use of military power in modern United States foreign policy. "One sees the influence of strategic culture in the use of military power in modern United States foreign policy, where advanced technology is emphasized and minimizing casualties is an operational limitation."[38]

It is a critical time in our nation's history and its emerging dialogue about the future state of the United States military during fiscally constrained times. The current long-term direction of United States fiscal policy is inconsistent with, and could ultimately undermine, America's national security. "A heavily debt-laden, over-obligated, revenue –squeezed government, highly dependent on foreign capital, creates major security vulnerabilities."[39]

Regardless of the past and what is to come in the future: "The American way of war remains a hybrid of European modes and something far more improvisational, far less rule-bound."[40]

China and War – More Art than Science

The Chinese military classics saw war as the means for "the preservation or the restoration of the perceived cosmological and moral order which the empire embodied, whether it was threatened by external enemies or internal rebels."[41] "For that reason, ancient China's unity or disunity was inextricably linked with the military world. The military was the force which delivered unity or disunity and in the process determined the integrity of China."[42]

As to the conduct of war, in contrast to modern European nation-states that controlled small territories and saw the annihilation of the enemy as a sensible way to secure state security, in China's vast multi-ethnic empire it made more sense to seek the incorporation of warrior peoples on the frontier, to appease them through trade, or to build frontier defenses, and to opt for their destruction only as a last resort.[43] "In spite of all the violence and warfare of China's history, the cultural legacy of antiquity made the significance of things military different from what it was in Byzantium or the Latin West."[44]

Unlike the United States, the Chinese do not openly publish their national security and military strategies. Commencing in the year 1998, the Chinese have published White Papers on their national military strategy and their modernization efforts. *China's National Defense in 2010* is the most recently published document on military and national security efforts. These documents provide an insight into Chinese current military planning and strategy but not the underpinnings to their overall philosophy of war. "To some extent this was because Chinese society did not produce people like Caesar or Thucydides – people who were chroniclers of warfare but also active participants."[45] "There is no denying that Chinese materials tend to be less informative about weapons, tactics, and details of combat than battle accounts from, say, Greece, Rome, Byzantium,"[46] or the United States.

"The Chinese are an ideologically based culture deeply rooted in history and tradition."[47] Concepts of war from historical writings such as Sun Tzu and modern theories of Chinese national leaders are key components of any analysis of the subject. China views itself as a civilization and not merely as a nation-state. It sees itself as a civilization that is destined to civilize the rest of the world.

China's National Defense in 2010 states; "The international situation is currently undergoing profound and complex changes. The progress toward economic globalization and a multi-polar world is irreversible, as is the advance toward informationization of society."[48] So China is announcing it arrival as a key player on the world stage. China is the latest club member to the classic rising power story, but has taken a revolutionary approach never seen before. It has placed everything in the prosperity basket while espousing economic reform under continued tight political control within the dictatorial power of a Communist State. "Elements within the Chinese policy community, and within its increasingly nationalistic population, believe that the United States is already pursuing 'containment' and that China's only option is to arm itself and challenge the United States."[49]

President Clinton's economic policy that brought China into the World Trade Organization had a subversive intent.

> China's political regime emphasized social order over individual rights, under enlargement America's chief goal then would be to establish a free-market economy and to assume that the rule of law and economic freedom, required for capitalism to flourish, would eventually work their way into China's political system.[50]

"The Chinese have been shrewd practitioners of *Realpolitik* and students of a strategic doctrine distinctly different from the strategy and diplomacy that found favor in the West."[51] The hallmark of *Realpolitik* is that it eschews ideological notions or moralistic or ethical premises. "The Chinese are less interested in Western linear thinking and logic than in gut feelings and their periodic, highly emotional assertion of their inalienable rights and dominance based on a culture that is over 5,000 years old."[52] That is why it is critical to also reflect on our competitor's beliefs about war.

"Chinese thinkers developed strategic thought that placed a premium on victory through psychological advantage and preached the avoidance of direct conflict."[53] Sun Tzu in his masterpiece treatise on "The Art of War," extolled the virtues of the psychological fight versus the force on force fight. The "Art of War" provides the basic concepts that shaped warfare in pre-modern China, Japan, Vietnam, and Korea. "Even today, the strategic patterns based on Sun Tzu's writing are deeply embedded in the military thinking of the sinicized Asian nations."[54]

His primary strategy was to win the fight without a fight. The Acme of Strategy for Sun Tzu was not to fight. "To subdue the enemy without fighting is the acme of skill."[55] To him it was all about shaping conditions. "Pretend inferiority and encourage his arrogance."[56] And when the conditions are set, move from this perceived position of weakness and strike.

Elements of this Sun Tzu philosophy, which have seen a modern revival of interest in China equivalent to the Clausewitz revival after World War II for the United States, can be seen in their economic practices. "Today, Sun Tzu is a lively topic at the Chinese National Defense University, and recent editions of Sun Tzu have been published by the People's Liberation Army's publishing company with the express purpose of educating officers in Sun Tzu's military art."[57]

Sun Tzu's military philosophy carried China through two thousand years of Imperial Rule which ended with the start of the "foreign occupation" in what the Chinese remember as a "century of humiliation". During those two thousand years of authoritarian rule China saw itself go through a cycles of unity and disunity and the military was there to maintain its integrity as a culture and as a nation.

The century of foreign occupation and the start of China's modern history can be traced back to the start of the Sino-British "Opium War", which was a trade war, in 1839 that ended with the signing of the Treaty of Nanjing in 1842.

> The Sino-British "Opium War" was significant for three reasons. One, it was arguably the first direct military conflict between a western European nation and China. Two, it was one of the first military conflicts in history to take advantage of the rapid technological changes that had gone hand-in-hand with British industrialization—such as compartmentalized metal ships and percussion rifles—thus setting a new standard for military conflicts. Three, the war ended when China agreed to sign an international treaty. This treaty was arguably the first that China ever signed in which the Chinese government accorded equal treatment to foreign participants—traditionally thought of as mere "barbarians.[58]

The next significant event in modern Chinese warfare was the Sino-Japanese War (1894-1895). The significance of this is that a small Asian nation comparable to the vastness of China was able to win and partition away Chinese territory through military superiority. The Japanese demands included claims to Korea, Taiwan, and Manchuria.

This partitioning of China was a first in Chinese history and led to the further process of foreign power partitioning of China.

The Boxer Uprising (1897-1900) was atypical of any other conflict In Chinese warfare history because there was a domestic element combined with an anti-foreign (imperialist) war. Additionally, the participants made extensive use of both traditional and modern military method combined with elements of magic and rituals. The Boxer Uprising was a watershed moment in Chinese military development. It deserves special attention because it represents "the last major retreat in China's path toward military modernization."[59] "China's military modernization had begun much earlier, but the appearance of the Boxers represented a temporary retreat from this modernization."[60] Therefore, "the only road left open to China after the Boxers was to modernize and adopt western methods."[61]

It was not surprising then that "western sinology grew accustomed to scrutinizing a China that was militarily weak and technologically backward, the hapless victim of Western and Japanese imperialists."[62] "Stated in the bluntest terms, China appeared to be a perennial loser with little to teach the winners when it came to the military arts."[63]

After nearly a century of foreign invasions and divided by its own civil wars, the once diverse and expansive China would not be reunited until the Red Army's victory over the Nationalist forces. The Nationalist Party and the Chinese Communist Party (CCP) renewed their ongoing civil war during 1946. "This conflict ended in 1949 with the creation of the People's Republic of China (PRC) and the removal of the Nationalist government to Taiwan."[64]

It is well know that Mao Zedong's military doctrine, known as the "people's war," became part of modern Chinese military thinking.

> At the heart of Mao's thought was the idea that human beings—or the "human factor"-- could "substitute for both the quantity and quality of the opponent's weapons," and that the outcome of a military conflict will be decided by "properly mobilized and politically motivated soldiers, fighting in accordance with the correct strategy and tactics."[65]

This is what propelled the Red Army to victory and the formation of the People's Liberation Army. This also established an enduring distrust of United States intentions in regards to its China policy because of its failed backing of Chiang Kai-shek and his Nationalist party.

After the People's Republic of China was established in 1949, it wasn't long before China's regional interests resurfaced. China's support to the Democratic People's Republic of Korea during the Korean War (1950-1953) against the United States and the United Nations Coalition Forces secured a military armistice. China's support was a cautionary countermeasure against the United States Cold War crusade against communism. China did not want to become the United States' next battleground against communism. "Regionally, the Korean War allowed China to reassert its historic claim of being the central power in Asia. Not only was the truce hailed as a great victory, but Beijing was now universally accepted as one of the major powers responsible for managing the Korean question."[66]

Territorial dispute issues led to the Sino-Indian border war (1962) that sent a clear signal to the world that China was determined to reclaim control over its lost territories. The Sino-Soviet territorial conflict (1969) although it ended in a stalemate essentially broke the yoke of communist ideological control away from Russia, reinforced China's military might, and sent a warning message to Vietnam "that they

18

should not try to challenge China's authority in Asia."[67] Regardless of the warning message sent in 1969, it did not prevent the Sino-Vietnamese conflict (1979). The consequence of the Soviets failure to support Vietnam and their newly signed Mutual Defense Treaty (1978) gave China the confidence to end the 1950 Sino-Soviet Treaty of Friendship, Alliance, and Mutual Assistance. The results of this conflict firmly entrenched China as an Asian power. However, China's experience in the 1979 Sino-Vietnamese conflict proved a military modernization program was needed. The architect of China's economic reform Deng Xiaoping also would lead the efforts for "comprehensive People's Liberation Army reforms on three different levels: (1) modernization of weapons, (2) streamlining and restructuring the officer corps, and (3) restoring political control over the PLA."[68]

During China's regional resurgence in Asia after the establishment of the People's Republic of China, Mao Zedong in 1966 imposed the "Cultural Revolution" to reassert his control over the communist party which he had lost to Chinese communist party moderates, like Deng Xiaoping, after his "Great Leap Forward" industrialization effort failed. The Cultural Revolution goals were to reeducate capitalists, intellectuals and eliminate the traditional elements of Chinese culture. The impact of the Cultural Revolution was disastrous because in essence you had the intelligent and most progressive elements of Chinese society being reeducated by the uneducated peasants of the Chinese countryside. This can be considered nothing short of a lost decade in China's development and diplomatic re-engagement with the United States.

Mao's ideological approach had failed. Deng Xiaoping saw the economic condition of the Chinese people needed improvement. Deng Xiaoping crafted the policies that would bring economic reform and also satisfy the Party's elders.

Despite the benefits of economic improvements and the growing prosperity of the Chinese there was no comparable political reform in the country. The Chinese Communist Party was still in control and was zealously repressing any dissent. The Tiananmen Massacre in June 1989 tainted the image of the Communist party and the Chinese Army from people's liberator institutions to the country's repressive watchdogs. This brought to the forefront the symbiotic relationship of the Chinese military security apparatus that keeps the Communist regime in power. Repression proved effective because it encouraged everyone else to keep quite. Once again, the cycle repeats itself and it is the military that maintains the integrity of China.

"It is the areas of economics and development that China has most vigorously exercised its soft power muscles, where the 'mutual benefit' is most apparent, and where the United States should be most wary of losing influence."[69]

China leverages inconsistencies in World Trade Organization rules and regulations to drive their economic engine at the expense of the United States creating trade friction. United States businesses and politicians accuse China of currency market manipulations in contravention of existing market rates through value suppression of the Chinese Yuan.

China is attempting to leverage sole source consumer streams of raw material from Africa and South America. China has cornered 97% of the rare earth elements market that is vital to our technologically driven world, and is the necessary raw material

element in the U.S. technologically superior military arsenal. As the United States'
"economic condition and financial institutions strengthened, so did its capacity to
mobilize the immense sums necessary for war."[70] The same corollary can now be
deduced for China as its economic power continues to grow. With economic power
comes the ability to grow a modern technologically advanced military that can have
global reach to protect what it now considers as its expanded "contested zone".

There are currently "three schools of thought in China today that analyze likely
wars and recommend what types of preparation China should undertake."[71] These three
schools of thought are identified as the People's War School, Local War School, and the
Revolution in Military Affairs Advocates.[72]

The first is Mao Zedong "People's War" which relies heavily upon the Chinese
masses to provide the human wave to oppose any force that wants to fight a land war in
China. The people's war school scenario envisions a direct invasion of China and a
protracted war to expel the invaders much like Mao Zedong had fought with the
Japanese. Just as in its original war of resistance, "China's area of interest can be
geographically divided into two areas, a defensive zone and that of contested zones."[73]
The defensive zone is defined as within the borders of China and includes those long
ago partitioned territories relinquished as the result of foreign invasion. The reversion of
Hong Kong from British to Chinese control in 1997 with the promise of "One Country,
Two Systems" and shortly thereafter the reversion of Macau from Portugal in 1999 were
watershed moments in China's reunification efforts. However, the continuing dispute
over Taiwan and its bid for self-determination remains for China the last major obstacle
to complete "peaceful" or "by force" reunification. This is also an enduring friction point

between China and the United States as the United States continues to support Taiwan against China's assertion that this is purely an internal matter. For proponents of the people's war school of thought, the Taiwan issue would be a possible flashpoint scenario. Nonetheless, Chinese military trends indicate more effort and thought is devoted to the second school of thought.

The Local War school of thought is the second of three schools of thought. This school of thought is one that focuses on transformation from a large standing Army to a smaller more lethal technological focused force that has rapid deployment capability. Deng Xiaoping is credited for articulating the initial conceptual framework that this school of thought espouses. The size and scope of war can involve anything short of global or nuclear conflict. It envisions a quick war that is near its borders. It envisions a rapid deployable military able to defeat any neighboring countries military forces the same as the United States did against Iraq during the Persian Gulf War (1990-1991). This school of thought would support what Mao Zedong labeled as the contested zone. This second area of China's geographic interests is best exemplified by the previous discussions on the Sino-Indian border war, the Sino-Soviet territorial disputes, and the Sino-Vietnamese conflict. The Local War school of thought would be vocal adherents to this viewpoint.

However, the third and newest school of thought advocates a Revolution in Military Affairs, calls "for development of offensive capabilities that can challenge American supremacy."[74] This is the most dangerous threat to the United States. A manifesto by two adherents to this school of thought has drawn attention in Western Circles. The 1999 book "*Unrestricted Warfare: China's Master Plan to Destroy America*"

22

written by senior Colonels Qia Liang and Wang Xiangsui of the People's Liberation Army advocates simply "Victory by any Means".[75] Some of these forms of unrestricted warfare can be financial, technological, control of natural resources, cyber, and economic. For instance in technology, the development of space capabilities matches or exceeds those of the United States because members of this school envision a future war with the Americans and they champion a globally offensive posture.[76]

The capability to launch these asymmetrical threats is a growing reality because of the economic powerhouse that China has become. Currently, estimates are that China has spent $90 billion in 2011 growing its military.[77] "These expenditures mask a much higher number estimated by the United States Department of Defense at double the highly publicized figure."[78]

There is natural evolution of thought when a nation now has global "vital" interests well beyond its borders that for its own continued preservation it must have the ability to protect those now crucial interests.

> A large nation will not only be more nearly certain to resist so direct an offense as invasion of its own borders, but, depending on its sense of power and importance, it will also commit itself to war or warlike acts over a broader spectrum of what it asserts to be provocations, which is to say simply that it interprets more expansively its "vital interests."[79]

The revolution in military affairs school of thought advances a strategic approach that is vital to the defense of China's international interests that can be protected through a capable military leveraging asymmetrical means. This school of thought recognizes that "China is in long-term competition with other major powers."[80]

As China increasingly builds its modern rapid deployable military capability to respond to what it will identify as provocative acts in its contested zones. It will begin to react more frequently to protect her interests. American's preferred method of victory during war through annihilation remains China's antithesis and remain consistent with Sun Tzu's observations. China will not in the near term openly risk its state or search for the annihilation of another. It will follow Sun Tzu and its history that "Generally in war the best policy is to take a state intact; to ruin it is inferior to this."[81] Additionally, attrition to the point of exhaustion is also too high a price to pay. "China intends to be a world military power and it spends like one."[82] China's has already taken its initial steps on its journey of a thousand miles to become a superpower.

Significance of the Two War Cultures on Bilateral Relations

"We do not have a choice on whether we will deal with China, but we do have a choice on how we deal with China."[83] The United States has discounted for too long the presence of Chinese interventionism in the Asia-Pacific region particularly during the Korean and Vietnam wars and now the United States is faced with China's increased global presence. An economy that has grown in the last two decades to become the second largest and strongest economy behind the United States with the potential to surpass the United States as the Gross Domestic Product Leader. Despite China's receiving most-favored nation trading status, U.S.-China relations remain constantly unsettled.[84] China's growing global economic influence will only multiply the chances for points of friction to occur leading to potential military confrontations. It is a widely held that economic ties will continue to grow even as we become increasingly military rivals. However, the United States must understand that a foreign economic policy with China is simply one element of a complete foreign policy, and it is certainly not a national security strategy.[85] Our foreign policy must be guided by a comprehensive grand strategy for engaging with China and must utilize all the tools available in the foreign policy toolkit. Our grand strategy should not be influenced by special Interests as it was

24

during the Clinton Administration. In 1993, then President Clinton linked trade relations with China to Human Rights, it was just a year later that he then reversed himself because of pressure from business interests and China. We haven't looked back since.

An understanding of global Chinese political, military, and economic intentions is vital for the development of a United States grand strategy to cope with the rise of China. China still poses no direct conventional military threat to our national security which could cause the annihilation or subjugation of our democratic nation. However, their growing asymmetrical capabilities in anti-satellite technology, anti-access doctrine, cyber warfare expertise, a growing missile arsenal and submarine fleet can only have a dampening effect on any United States military operations such as AirSea Battle in close proximity of China's sphere of influence. The asymmetrical capability threat is a cause for concern that will be exacerbated ultimately by a globally capable Chinese military that by some estimates is only a decade away.

We are entering a bi-polar and possibly a multi-polar world fraught with risk. The bi-polar world is one similar to the Cold War model where there are two blocs of power with developed spheres of influence around the globe. Then it was the United States and the Soviets, and the one emerging now envisions the United States and China as the next two blocs of power vying for influence in the world. However, China's view is of a multi-polar world where the United States, Brazil, Russia, India, and China wield power and influence in the world. What lies ahead is unfamiliar territory for the United States and China because in either model of polarity both of these countries are key actors in either world. What is the optimum engagement approach to prevent a competitor to switch and become an adversary? Chinese strategy avoids direct confrontation against America's strengths, but does seek out the seams in order to exploit our weaknesses through asymmetric means.

To oversimplify the different characteristics of how the two nation's war cultures play out on the world's stage visualize two opponents facing each other across the Hasbro strategic board game of "Risk". The board game allows for 2-6 players at any given time. So, it can emulate a bipolar or a multi-polar world. In today's risk game there are two players, the first player is Uncle Sam representing the United States and the second player sitting across from him is a Dragon representing China. The objective of the game remains the same for "conquest of the world" or "world domination". However, due to the cultural differences of the players, today's rules are modified so the player can use the rules of their respective intellectual games favored by their culture. Uncle Sam will use chess strategies and the Dragon will use China's game *wei qi* strategies or "go" as it is known to westerners. "*Wei qi* translates as 'a game of surrounding pieces'; it implies a concept of strategic encirclement."[86] These national games and their rules are emblematic of how these two powers would execute military strategies over the global map.

Uncle Sam immediately goes about the task of placing all his chess pieces on the map in linear formations with many of them forward projected. The hierarchy of the pieces and their placement signifies the political and military importance of that region of the world to United States strategic interests. All these chess pieces (resources) are prepared to sacrifice the pawns in order to attrite and annihilate the opponent pieces to achieve a decisive win. Uncle Sam operates on the premise "If I have a higher body count than you, then I must be winning". Now, the Dragon does something that perplexes Uncle Sam and places a single "go" stone in areas of the world like Africa, South America, and throughout Asia but keeps the majority of the stones in the cup nestled close to him. To Uncle Sam there is no rhyme or reason to this individual placement of stones but to the Dragon all the stones are working as they should for the strategic purpose they were placed. As the Dragon continues to place more stones on the open spaces on the board avoiding direct confrontation with Uncle Sam's chess pieces, suddenly Uncle Sam finds that he is slowly being encircled and out maneuvered and his concerns grow because he sees that there is now competition for many spaces on the board. Yet, Uncle Sam is unable to react because he has committed and in some cases over committed resources to address actively contested spaces on the board that are currently more vital to his current strategic interests. This oversimplification stresses the differences in thought patterns. "Chess produces single-mindedness; *wei qi* generates strategic flexibility."[87]

How do you cross the bridge to think like your enemy? "Strategists who are forced to undertake the uncomfortable task of planning operations against opponents of a different culture"[88]-- do so at their own risk if they do not become students of that culture. So, the best approach may be to find the commonalties which may be more readily achievable as China takes a more western approach on the matter of war. For instance, despite the differences, in both cultures, "generals sought to postpone engagements until the time was ripe, to increase the likelihood of success through artful maneuver or clever stratagems."[89]

Let's take the approach of artful maneuver. "While the Chinese may be lowballing their estimates and definitely their ambitions, it seems unlikely that they can indefinitely keep up their economic success, which is the foundation for their military development and modernization."[90] What are the implications for the United States?

We must believe in the nation-to-nation dialogue started on 14 February 2012 between President Obama and Chinese Vice President Xi Jinping with a focus on cooperation. At the outset, this good beginning is good for the two nations and ostensibly, the rest of the world. A strong U.S.-China bilateral relationship creates a stabilizing force between these two global powers with an emphasis on their ability to air differences without blame through the art of negotiation and dialogue. The United States should take a *RealPolitik* approach to our relations with China. The United States when its serves its interests disregards its values which creates a strategic communication's gap between what it says and what it does. In the information battle space strategic communication is vital to the development of trust and respect. For the United States,

> Strategic communication refers to focused USG efforts to understand and engage key audiences to create, strengthen, or preserve conditions favorable for the advancement of USG interests, policies, and objectives through the use of coordinated programs, plans, themes, messages, and products synchronized with and leveraging the actions of all instruments of national power.[91]

The United States overriding interest is a healthy relationship with China that is mutually beneficial to each other and the world. Yet, the inconsistency between words and deeds of the United States cultivate a climate of uncertainty and fear. It's time to apply political pragmatism. The United States must develop a carefully designed strategy on China that accepts that we're dealing with a Communist system that has adopted market capitalism, and consumerism. The United States picks and chooses when and where Human Rights abuse issues affect international policy. The ship has sailed on human rights when it comes to China and is not returning. Why the continued support of Taiwan and concern for its democratic way of life when the United States has consistently supported totalitarian regimes throughout its modern history because it served its interests to do so? Equally, China should be fully included in all discussions on the future of the Koreas which would dissipate some of the distrust still fermenting over that unresolved issue.

The United States must center on a dialogue that focuses on trust and respect that creates a bilateral and regional sense of security where there are no perceptions of threats and each nation's motives are transparent. This is particularly needed when we start new strategic posturing that could be viewed by China as an attempt at containment. "Sustained and reliable United States-China military-to-military relations support this goal by reducing mistrust, enhancing mutual understanding and broadening cooperation."[92]

The concerns already exist and have sparked a spurt on China's development of asymmetrical weapons technologies to battle the perceived threat of AirSea battle doctrine. Wouldn't it be pragmatic to agree to a mutual restraint on new weapon capability developments reinforced by diplomatic assurances of our intentions not to destabilize their government? Wouldn't it be preferential to agree on mutual cooperation on cyber security and trade and economics?

We used the same approach when Japan was emerging as a regional economic power and just like Japan and South Korea a strong and prosperous China is one that can bring stability and prosperity to Asia-Pacific region and the world. We must engage China on Asia Pacific issues before they become crises particularly where China is a party to a regional dispute. Engagement is the best approach for the United States with

China in determining the true intentions of the Chinese. It is critical that we develop a cooperative security program with the Chinese.

Conclusion

The purpose of this paper was to analyze United States and China relations through the lens of strategic war cultures and to reveal the unique dissimilarities of American and Chinese warfare and to determine if it has an impact on the way these rival nations interact. Overall the American and Chinese way of war is a byproduct of America's and China's unique cultural and political traditions, value systems, and historical lessons as found in historical and contemporary strategic documents.[93]

The analysis covered the development of warfare in America through an historical lens from it birth as a nation through to the Gulf War. Similarly, we went through a brief history of warfare in China with a focused effort on the history of "modern" China which started with the foreign occupation of China through to Tiananmen Square. Each nation's military history is distinctive.

Furthermore, there was an assessment to the current diplomatic, military, and economic implications of continued interaction between these two nations. It is essential information in the development of a conceptual basis to set United States future engagement strategy upon.

The study of the American and Chinese way of war is important today because of its implications to the United States due to the global role that these two countries have in the international arena tethered to the growing concern that the evolving distrust between them will eventually lead to a military confrontation. The United States has the world's foremost military in the world while China has the largest military in the world. The United States has increased its focus on homeland security, maintenance and strengthening of its regional influence particularly in the Asia-Pacific region and the continued protection and preservation of its global interests. China's focus continues to remain on internal security and expansion of its regional influence but is expanding to a strategic outlook for the protection and promotion of its global interests.[94] This now creates situations fraught with risk as we begin to operate in similar spaces.

Whether future engagements come as a cooperative partnership or in an adversarial environment, we must "encourage China to make choices that contribute to peace, security, and prosperity as its influence rises."[95] Economic relations between the United States and China continue to grow while the political and military relations continue to be inconsistent and often duplicate the tense patterns of distrust during the Cold War era. Globalization has become the bane of everyone's existence since no longer can one retreat from the world without being impacted. As the United States and China international leadership roles become increasingly interdependent, the imperative to understand each other grows. These two global powers, whether friend or foe, need to understand each other's worlds and do more listening versus talking past each other. Strategic principles of war do have an influence on diplomatic, military, and economic strategy development. It is critical for United States strategic planners across the elements of power to study the Chinese way of war as their concept of war evolves for the 21st century. Simply, we cannot afford to idly standby waiting for the next crisis to determine whether we're in danger and in need of a grand strategy to address China. The United States is more focused on overwhelming military power, China on decisive psychological impact. Sooner or later, one side or the other will miscalculate.[96] It must be recognized that "this is a power tango and it's far from predetermined who in the circle will hold the rose in their teeth."[97]

Endnotes

[1] Robert B. Strassler, ed., The Landmark Thucydides: A Comprehensive Guide To The Peloponnesian War (New York, Free Press, 1996), 16.

[2] Henry Kissinger, On China. (New York: The Penguin Press, 2011), 493.

[3] Mark A. Stoler, George C. Marshall: Soldier-Statesman of the American Century. (Boston, MA: Twayne Publishers, 1989), 53.

[4] David Lai, The United States and China in Power Transition (Carlisle Barracks, PA: U.S. Army War College, Strategic Studies Institute, December 2011), 53.

[5] Kissinger, On China, 520.

[6] Nicholas R. Krueger, The Rationale for a Robust U.S. Army Presence in the Pacific Basin. (Arlington, VA., AUSA Institute of Land Warfare National Security Watch 12-2, March 8, 2012), 5.

[7] Ben Lombardi, "Assumptions and Grand Strategy" Parameters 41, no.1 (Spring 2011): 37.

[8] Richard D. Lewis, When Cultures Collide: Leading Across Cultures, 3rd ed. (Boston, MA; Nicholas Brealey International, 2006), 485.

[9] Ibid, 485.

[10] Kathleen D. Cole, The Sleeping Dragon Awakens: Ramifications of Chinese Influence in Latin America, Strategy Research Project (Carlisle Barracks, PA: U.S. Army War College, March 10, 2006), 4.

[11] Peter D. Kiernan, Becoming China's Bitch: and Nine More Catastrophes We Must Avoid Right Now. (New York: Turner Publishing Company, 2012), 174.

[12] Barack Obama, National Security Strategy (Washington, DC: The White House, May 2010), 43.

[13] Anatol Lieven, Pakistan: A Hard Country. (New York: PublicAffairs, 2011), 44.

[14] Kiernan, Becoming China's Bitch: and Nine More Catastrophes We Must Avoid Right Now, 176.

[15] George C. Herring, America's Longest War: The United States and Vietnam, 1950-1975, 4th ed. (New York, McGraw Hill, 2002), ix.

[16] Eliot A. Cohen, Conquered Into Liberty. (New York: Free Press, 2011), 70.

[17] Russell F. Weigley, The American Way of War: A History of United States Military Strategy and Policy. (Bloomington, IN: Indiana University Press, 1973), xxi.

[18] Ibid, 88.

[19] Michael Howard and Peter Paret, eds. and trans, Carl von Clausewitz, On War (Princeton, NJ: Princeton University Press, 1976), 75.

[20] Weigley, The American Way of War: A History of United States Military Strategy and Policy, xx.

[21] Ibid, xxii.

[22] Ibid, xxi.

[23] Howard and Paret, Carl von Clausewitz, On War, 87.

[24] Michael Howard, Clausewitz, A Very Short Introduction (Oxford, UK: Oxford University Press, 1983), 45.

[25] Milan Vego, "On Military Theory," Joint Forces Quarterly, Issue 62 (3rd Quarter 2011): 60.

[26] Howard and Paret, Carl von Clausewitz, On War, 87.

[27] James M. Dubik, LTG (Ret), "Asia-Pacific First: What Does this Actually Mean?" Army Magazine Vol. 62, no.2 (February 2012): 20.

[28] Herring, America's Longest War, ix.

[29] David Lai, Learning from the Stones: A Go Approach to Mastering China's Strategic Concept, Shi (Carlisle Barracks, PA: U.S. Army War College, Strategic Studies Institute, March 10, 2004), 27.

[30] Ibid, 2.

[31] Dennis Steele, "Strategic Reset" Army Magazine Vol. 62, no.3 (March 2012): 58.

[32] Ibid, 58.

[33] U.S. Joint Chiefs of Staff, The National Military Strategy of the United States of America, 2011, Redefining America's Military Leadership (Washington, DC: Joint Chiefs of Staff, February 8, 2011), 8.

[34] Consulate General of the United States Hong Kong & Macau Official Web Portal, As Delivered by Admiral Mike Mullen, chairman Joint Chiefs of Staff, New Delhi, India Friday, July 23, 2010, http://hongkong.usconsulate.gov/uscn_dod_2010072301.html (accessed February 28, 2012).

[35] Paul Oh, "Assessing Chinese Intentions for the Military Use of the Space Domain," Joint Forces Quarterly, Issue 64 (1st Quarter 2012): 97.

[36] JoAnne Wagner, "Going Out: Is China's Skillful Use of Soft Power in Sub-Saharan Africa a Threat to U.S. Interests?," Joint Forces Quarterly, Issue 64 (1st Quarter 2012): 104.

[37] U.S. Joint Chiefs of Staff, The National Military Strategy of the United States of America, 2011, Redefining America's Military Leadership, 14.

[38] Ben Lombardi, "Assumptions and Grand Strategy," 35.

[39] Robert D. Hormats, The Price of Liberty: Paying For America's Wars From The Revolution To The War On Terror. (New York: Henry Holt and Company, LLC, 2007), xxi.

[40] Cohen, Conquered Into Liberty, 340.

[41] Hans Van De Ven, ed., Warfare in Chinese History (Leiden, Brill, 2000), 9.

[42] Diana Lary, "Defending China: The Battles of the Xuzhou Campaign" in Warfare in Chinese History, ed. Hans Van De Ven, (Leiden, Brill, 2000), 398.

[43] Van De Ven, Warfare in Chinese History, 10.

[44] David A. Graff, Medieval Chinese Warfare, 300-900. (London: Routledge, 2002), 256.

[45] Ibid, 7.

[46] Ibid, 7.

[47] Cole, The Sleeping Dragon Awakens: Ramifications of Chinese Influence in Latin America, 1.

[48] Chinese Government's Official Web Portal, China's National Defense in 2010, http://www.china.org.cn/government/whitepaper/node_7114675.htm (accessed February 27, 2012).

[49] David J. Greene, "U.S. Strategy in Southeast Asia: Power Broker, Not Hegemon," Joint Forces Quarterly, Issue 64 (1st Quarter 2012): 132.

[50] Stephen E. Ambrose and Douglas G. Brinkley, Rise to Globalism: American Foreign Policy since 1938. (London: Penguin Books, 1997), 407.

[51] Kissinger, On China, 22.

[52] Lewis, When Cultures Collide: Leading Across Cultures, 47.

[53] Kissinger, On China, 25.

[54] Edward O'Dowd and Arthur Waldron, "Sun Tzu for Strategists" Comparative Strategy Vol. 10, no.1 (1991): 25.

[55] Samuel B Griffith, Sun Tzu: The Art of War. (London: Oxford University Press, 1963), 77.

[56] Ibid, 67.

[57] O'Dowd and Waldron, "Sun Tzu for Strategists", 26.

[58] Bruce A. Elleman, Modern Chinese Warfare, 1795-1989 (London: Routledge, 2001), 13.

[59] Ibid, 116.

[60] Ibid, 137.

[61] Ibid, 137.

[62] David A. Graff, Medieval Chinese Warfare, 300-900. (London: Routledge, 2002), 1.

[63] Ibid, 1.

[64] Elleman, Modern Chinese Warfare, 217.

[65] Ibid, 304.

[66] Ibid, 253.

[67] Ibid, 280.

[68] Ibid, 304.

[69] Wagner, "Going Out: Is China's Skillful Use of Soft Power in Sub-Saharan Africa a Threat to U.S. Interests?," 101.

[70] Hormats, The Price of Liberty: Paying For America's Wars From The Revolution To The War On Terror, xiv.

[71] Michael Pillsbury, "China Debates the Future Security Environment, Chapter 6, Forecasting Future Wars," January 2000. http://www.au.af.mil/au/awc/awcgate/ndu/chindebate/pills2.htm#CDFch6. (accessed April 14, 2012).

[72] Ibid

[73] Tony K. Cho, "Mao's War of Resistance: Framework for China's Grand Strategy" Parameters 41, no.3 (Autumn 2011): 10.

[74] Oh, "Assessing Chinese Intentions for the Military Use of the Space Domain", 94.

[75] Qiao Liang and Wang Xiangsui, Unrestricted Warfare: China's Master Plan to Destroy America, Panama City, Panama: Pan American Publishing Company, 2002.

[76] Oh, "Assessing Chinese Intentions for the Military Use of the Space Domain", 95.

[77] Kiernan, Becoming China's Bitch: and Nine More Catastrophes We Must Avoid Right Now, 174.

[78] Ibid, 175.

[79] Bernard Brodie, War & Politics. (New York: Macmillan Publishing Co., Inc., 1973), 2.

[80] Michael Pillsbury, "China Debates the Future Security Environment, http://www.au.af.mil/au/awc/awcgate/ndu/chindebate/pills2.htm#CDFch6. (accessed April 14, 2012).

[81] Griffith, Sun Tzu: The Art of War, 77.

[82] Kiernan, Becoming China's Bitch: and Nine More Catastrophes We Must Avoid Right Now, 175.

[83] Daniel S. Larsen, "U.S.-China Relations: No Need to Fight," Joint Forces Quarterly, Issue 63 (4th Quarter 2011): 94.

[84] Ambrose and Brinkley, Rise to Globalism: American Foreign Policy since 1938, 413.

[85] Ibid, 403.

[86] Kissinger, On China, 23.

[87] Ibid, 25.

[88] O'Dowd and Waldron, "Sun Tzu for Strategists", 34.

[89] Graff, Medieval Chinese Warfare, 300-900, 255.

[90] Larsen, "U.S.-China Relations: No Need to Fight", 93.

[91] U.S. Joint Chiefs of Staff, Joint Operation Planning, Joint Publication 5-0 (Washington, DC: U.S. Joint Chiefs of Staff, August 11, 2011), II-9.

[92] Office of the Secretary of Defense, Military and Security Developments Involving the People's Republic of China: A Report to Congress Pursuant to the National Defense Authorization Act for Fiscal Year 2010 (Washington DC, U.S. Government Printing Office, 2010), I.

[93] James G. Pangelinan, "From Red Cliffs to Chosin: The Chinese Way of War, AY 2010. http://www.dtic.mil/cgi-bin/GetTRDoc?AD=ADA523450. (accessed April 14, 2012).

[94] Ibid.

[95] Obama, National Security Strategy, 43.

[96] Kissinger, On China, 521.

[97] Kiernan, Becoming China's Bitch: and Nine More Catastrophes We Must Avoid Right Now, 177.

www.ingramcontent.com/pod-product-compliance
Lightning Source LLC
Chambersburg PA
CBHW081804280526
45789CB00008B/2995